THE SCOOP ON POOP

POOP's Many Uses

by Ellen Lawrence

Consultant:
Garret Suen, Assistant Professor
Department of Bacteriology
University of Wisconsin
Madison, Wisconsin

BEARPORT
PUBLISHING

New York, New York

Credits

Cover, © wiwsphoto/Shutterstock, © Pat P/Shutterstock, and © Jeff Morgan/Alamy; 2, © xtock/Shutterstock; 4T, © Anan Kaewkhammul/Shutterstock; 4B, © toowaret/Shutterstock; 5, © Hemis/Alamy; 5BR, © xtock/Shutterstock; 6T, © Chonlatip Hirunsatitporn/Shutterstock; 6C, © Jeff Morgan/Alamy; 6B, © Jeff Morgan/Alamy; 7, © Jeff Morgan/Alamy; 7R, © Tomas Miki/Shutterstock; 7BR, © xtock/Shutterstock; 8, © Mike Roelofs; 9, © Ruud Balk; 10T, © Stef Bennett/Shutterstock; 10B, © fotojoost/Shutterstock; 11, © Lisa S./Shutterstock; 12, © Don Mammoser/Shutterstock; 13, © Jesse Kraft/Alamy; 14, © SOIL (Sustainable Organic Integrated Livelihoods); 15, © Jon Brack; 16T, © RGB Ventures/Superstock/Alamy; 16B, © W. Scott McGill/Shutterstock; 17, © Herschel Hoffmeyer/Shutterstock; 17TL, © Jennifer Lynch/Bella Diva Beads; 17BR, © Pooretat Moonsana/Shutterstock; 18T, © Nelson Akira Ishikawa/Shutterstock; 18B, © Alexander Mazurkevich/Shutterstock; 19, © kajornyot wildlife photography/Shutterstock; 19B, © Dima Sobko/Shutterstock; 20, © jiunn/Shutterstock, © zizi mentos/Shutterstock, and © FenixSPB/Shutterstock; 21, © NASA; 22, © jiunn/Shutterstock, © zizi mentos/Shutterstock, © Paula Photo/Shutterstock, © ksusha27/Shutterstock, and © Kamomeen/Shutterstock; 23TL, © Bene A/Shutterstock; 23TC, © filippo giuliani/Shutterstock; 23TR, © Quality Stock Images/Shutterstock; 23BL, © CHAINFOTO24/Shutterstock; 23BC, © Mike Roelofs; 23BR, © Jeff Morgan/Alamy.

Publisher: Kenn Goin
Editor: Jessica Rudolph
Creative Director: Spencer Brinker
Photo Researcher: Ruth Owen Books

Library of Congress Cataloging-in-Publication Data

Names: Lawrence, Ellen, 1967– author.
Title: Poop's many uses / by Ellen Lawrence.
Description: New York, New York : Bearport Publishing, [2018] | Series: The scoop on poop | Includes bibliographical references and index.
Identifiers: LCCN 2017014719 (print) | LCCN 2017021694 (ebook) | ISBN 9781684023028 (ebook) | ISBN 9781684022489 (library)
Subjects: LCSH: Animal droppings—Juvenile literature.
Classification: LCC QL768 (ebook) | LCC QL768 .L32 2018 (print) | DDC 591.47—dc23
LC record available at https://lccn.loc.gov/2017014719

For more information, write to Bearport Publishing Company, Inc., 45 West 21st Street, Suite 3B, New York, New York 10010. Printed in the United States of America.

10 9 8 7 6 5 4 3 2 1

Contents

Recycle Yucky Waste

When we hear the word *poop*, we usually think of smelly waste.

However, some **inventors** have discovered ways to **recycle** poop!

For example, most paper is made of **fibers** that come from the wood of trees.

Yet other plants contain fibers, too.

When animals eat grass, the fibers end up in their dung.

This means animal poop can also be made into paper—but how?

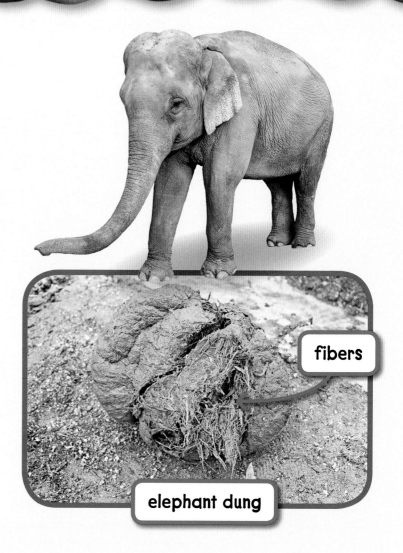

fibers

elephant dung

4

Paper can be made from the poop of many different plant-eating animals, including elephants and sheep.

elephant dung paper

How do you think a pile of sheep droppings is turned into paper?

5

Sheep Poop Paper

To make sheep poop paper, a farmer first collects the animal's dung.

Then he or she washes it in boiling water until only the fibers remain.

The fibers are mixed with other ingredients to create a mushy pulp.

The pulp is placed in trays and then crushed in a machine to remove all the water.

As the pulp is crushed, the fibers join together and form paper.

sheep poop

pulp

tray

a card made from sheep poop

sheets of paper drying

Sheep poop paper contains lots of fibers from the grass that the animals eat. The paper is made into items such as cards and bookmarks.

Why do you think it's a good idea to make paper from animal dung?
(See page 24 for possible answers.)

Poo Fashion

It's not only paper that can be made from animal dung.

A scientist and designer named Jalila Essaïdi has created a fabric from recycled cow manure.

She makes cow poop clothes!

Other people are inventing ways to make furniture, plates, and even cups from dung.

This work is very important because there's too much poop in the environment.

Jalila Essaïdi working on her invention

These models are wearing clothes made from cow dung.

Farm animals in the United States produce about 335 million tons (304 million metric tons) of manure each year. All this poop weighs about the same as 1,000 Empire State Buildings!

Too Much Dung

Around the world, farm animals produce billions of tons of dung each year.

This stinking waste is often left to rot in huge heaps.

It releases harmful gases into the air.

When it rains, the poop often gets washed into rivers, where it pollutes the water.

a heap of cow dung

Farmers recycle manure by spreading it on their fields as **fertilizer**. The manure helps their crops grow. However, farm animals produce so much dung that there's still lots left over.

manure

Guano Fertilizer

Bird poop, or guano, makes great fertilizer.

Many seabirds live in huge groups on small rocky islands.

Over time, some islands become covered with the birds' droppings.

For centuries, people in South America gathered guano from islands off the coast of Peru.

In the 1800s, traders came from the United States and Europe to buy shiploads of this guano fertilizer.

a rocky island off Peru's coast

Two hundred years ago, the guano on some islands near Peru was 150 feet (46 m) deep!

pelican

cormorant

guano

Helpful Human Poop

Human poop can also be used as fertilizer!

On a visit to Haiti, scientist Sasha Kramer saw that most people didn't have toilets.

They dumped waste near their homes or in rivers or the ocean.

Sasha designed toilets with waste containers that can be collected from homes each week.

Then the waste is taken to a recycling plant and turned into fertilizer for crops!

a recycling toilet

Sasha Kramer

fertilizer

People add materials such as sawdust to their waste. At the recycling plant, the mixture rots and gets very hot. The heat kills off harmful germs. After six months, the poop is ready to be used as fertilizer.

15

Prehistoric Poo

Dung doesn't have to be fresh to be useful.

Did you know dinosaur poop is used to make jewelry?

Over millions of years, chunks of dinosaur dung can turn into rocky **fossils** called coprolites.

Some coprolites are more than 150 million years old!

The dino doo-doo can be polished and used to make colorful necklaces and bracelets.

the inside of a coprolite

a dinosaur coprolite

a bracelet made
from coprolite beads

Prehistoric poop
often contains bits of
bones or plants. These
materials can tell scientists
what foods dinosaurs ate.

Can you guess what
drink is made from
this animal poop?

A Cup of Dung Coffee!

In Indonesia, the poop of small animals called civets is used to make coffee!

Civets eat the berries of coffee plants.

Each berry contains a seed, or coffee bean.

A civet **digests** the soft fruit and then poops out the hard beans.

People collect the beans, wash them, and grind them up to make civet coffee.

coffee berries

pooped-out coffee beans

a civet

Some people think coffee beans pooped by civets make a better-tasting coffee. Perhaps substances inside a civet's stomach change the beans' taste. No one knows for sure!

Outer Space Waste

Did you know scientists are also researching ways to recycle astronaut poop?

One day, astronauts may make long journeys to Mars and beyond.

In a small spacecraft, there's little room for supplies like food.

If astronauts could make meals from their recycled poop, this would help solve the issue.

This is a poopy science problem for the future!

An astronaut's supper is ready.

The astronaut poops.

The poop goes into a recycling machine.

The machine turns the poop into food.

Recycling Space Poop— could this be possible?

The astronauts aboard the International Space Station (ISS) already recycle their pee. It's cleaned by special equipment and turned back into drinking water.

These astronauts are drinking recycled urine!

21

Science Lab

What Would *You* Do With Astronaut Poo?

Scientists believe there are many ways that recycled astronaut waste could be used in the future.

Perhaps human waste could be made into a type of plastic. Then special equipment aboard a spacecraft could make screws and other spare parts from the plastic.

If you were a scientist, what would you do with astronaut poo?

Think about these questions as you brainstorm.

- **What things might an astronaut need on a long journey in space?**

- **What type of equipment would be needed to recycle the poo into something new?**

Draw a picture or diagram of your idea. Give your picture labels. Does your idea have a name?

Science Words

digests (dye-JESTS) breaks down food inside the digestive system

fertilizer (FUR-tuh-lize-ur) a substance added to soil to help plants grow better

fibers (FYE-burz) thin, string-like threads inside the leaves and stems of plants

fossils (FOSS-uhlz) the hard, rock-like remains of prehistoric animals and plants

inventors (in-VEN-turz) people who solve problems by designing or making new objects, or new ways to do things

recycle (ree-SYE-kuhl) to turn a used or unwanted thing or material into something new

Index

Read More

Goodman, Susan E.
The Truth About Poop.
New York: Viking (2004).

Graubart, Norman D. *How to Track a Black Bear (Scatalog: A Kid's Field Guide to Animal Poop).* New York: Windmill Books (2015).

Woolf, Alex. *You Wouldn't Want to Live Without Poop!* New York: Franklin Watts (2016).

Learn More Online

To learn more about poop's uses, visit **www.bearportpublishing.com/TheScoopOnPoop**

About the Author

Ellen Lawrence lives in the United Kingdom. Her favorite books to write are those about nature and animals. In fact, the first book Ellen bought for herself, when she was six years old, was the story of a gorilla named Patty Cake that was born in New York's Central Park Zoo.

Answer to Page 7

In order to make paper from wood, trees have to be cut down. Making paper from poop helps save trees. Also, animals such as sheep produce large quantities of poop every day. So, this waste material never runs out!